ZENTANGLED

KATHY V. KUZMA

authorHOUSE®

AuthorHouse™
1663 Liberty Drive
Bloomington, IN 47403
www.authorhouse.com
Phone: 833-262-8899

Published by AuthorHouse 09/27/2021

ISBN: 978-1-6655-3956-2 (sc)
ISBN: 978-1-6655-3955-5 (e)

Print information available on the last page.

*Any people depicted in stock imagery provided by Getty Images are models,
and such images are being used for illustrative purposes only.
Certain stock imagery © Getty Images.*

This book is printed on acid-free paper.

DEDICATION

I dedicate my book of poems to my mother and father,
Verla and Peter Schmidt.

They gave me the gift of imagination and appreciation of nature.

ZENTANGLE

Life patterns in a border,
Deliberate and conscious
But free and flowing,
Like the flutter of a curtain
As the breeze breathes,
The mind sleeps
And a dream begins.

Calm creativity in a form,
Soothing tangled lines
And twisted time
While details dance
In syncopated rhyme.
Heartbeats of the pen
In waltzing zen.

TIGHT

Squeezing her feet in her shoes,
She ran out the back door
Everything was tight,
From her skin to her clothes
She could fit through small spaces
Like a note slid under a door
A thin flying kite that could soar
We watched her through the years
Wondering if she was a sprite

It was a magical time of wonder
We believed in exuberance
She projected energy and joy
A walk in the woods alone,
In a tree climbing freedom zone
No fear of the sound of a gun
Just a back door slam as she ran
She embodied all that was right
Love, like her shoes and her life,
Interlaced, nice and tight

INSIDE\UNDER

Ketchup stuck inside the bottle
Gum found under the table
The flip side of a turning coin
The glue behind the label

Beneath the skin, a universe
Inside like popping bubbles
No one sees them bursting
They are all internal puzzles

Look right under the doormat
Turn any stone on its side
You'll find what's underneath
Everything tries to hide

TUBES

It streamed down the line
In clear liquid words,
But the final product
Was empty.
He did not see or hear
The drops,
Though transparent
And reiterated.

So many drips away
And still the tubes
Were full
Waiting...

Like frozen pipes
On a winter's day.

MELTDOWN

Waiting for an ice pack
To sooth the fevered few
A sip of cold surrender
The taste of no more lies
Frozen facts forthcoming
In a meltdown of the truth
Old men sliding downhill
False memories of their youth

Dripping dreams sputter
Like water down a spout
Captured in a bucket
Made of chewed up time
With pieces of tomorrow
A panoramic sight
Countdown til the morning
Hopeful...but not quite

DISINTER

A mud spattered sun
In the afternoon
A real life dilemma
Not just a cartoon

A soft haze gathered
Like butter on toast
With a touch of jam
Evening...almost

Rust colored skies
Lamps in the gloom
Make them brighter
Humanity...exhume

DETOURED

The pill settled down in the throat
Mixed in a maze of saliva
A liquid lozenge of delusion
It slipped like a loose tooth
Swallowed without wisdom
A vague triumph of tranquility
With a haze of propriety

The slurring surrender
Was a peaceful priority
Linked with a sip of syrup
That sweetened the trip
Like a closed country road
Just a temporary detour
Selfish... but secure

LOOK BELOW

Slow descent from the ladder,
Like planting seeds in soil
Cautious, careful bending
With dexterity and thought.
The prize below was simple
But the task above was not,
Like recalling so many faces
But the names - we forgot.

Now the world is slipping.
We missed the bottom step.
The upward climb was greedy.
We heard the call to stop,
A wise voice of conscience
That told us "look below."
Just tend to the garden
The ladder, we can forgo.

THE TRANSFER

Timid eyes squint and strain
But miss the dancing danger.
Specks spray like ballet twirls.
They land on slippery floors.
Pointed shoes direct the way
But the droplets do not stay.

They pass to partners,
Prance and spin,
Collide like acrobats.
The audience is unaware
The transfer has begun
And, for some, their dance
Is done!

LAST BREATH

The soft ripple from the chest,
Like a slow squeeze of the trigger,
As moments churn sideways.
An instant recall of the breath.
Acknowledgement of a ruse.
Time shifts
And a hollowness ensues.

Like missing the last step,
That free falling instant
When you know
A life has seeped away...
You see the emptiness,
A fallen petal
In a bouquet.

WAFT

The particles were invisible
But she saw them go
Like a breeze
That soothes a fever.
The flutter of a feather,
Innocuous in their flow.

She knew their destination,
A window wide and clear.
Like a smooth transition,
In a final waft of air.
Some gently drifted upward
But she kept the best...
Right here.

LAST CALL

In the back of the crowd,
A blue jacket emerged.
The color was moot.
It was the man inside.

The rabble roared
But the blue man sighed,
Like the last call in a bar,
With an empty glass.

Surrounded by fools,
Ignorance fed,
He shook his head.
Gestured integrity...
Enough unsaid!

NEAR

The traveller returned
In a near rhyme.
But that was wrong,
Like an unexpected slap.
What was once so far
Was now the noise of near.
That raucous note.
A halt in the air
When words flip.
A pause in time
With imperfect rhyme.

The heavy whisper,
Like a swallowed rock,
Pushed down deep
And settled
Near.
It all came back
And now was
Here.

REGRET

Open the door.
What secrets abide?
Dust and debris
on dancing shoes.
A tangled tango
of nerves inside.

Glaring graffiti
written in red,
like lipstick smeared
over words not said.

A life not spent.
Perfume that lingers
in an empty room.
All that's left
is the fragrant scent.

REALITY

The dog barked incessantly,
Like a siren in the night.
It is the sound of waiting,
A stretching of time
From silence to insanity.

That faraway call.
Humanity howls
In sadness or in pain
Just a shadowy shroud
To catch us when we fall.

Deja vu of all we feel
A wailing wall of wounds
Darkness we know well.
We hear it in our sleep
Reminders…
Life is real

LOST GOLD

Escape was convoluted.
Complicated chaos
But necessary mindfulness,
Because the dream was real,
Like the lost art of alchemy.
Transformation you can feel.

The world had shuddered,
Trembling turmoil.
Base metal instead of gold.
There had to be more,
So we transcended,
Tiptoed out...

And shut the door!

SLIP SLIDING

Like the waning moon,
Cycles of life
Constantly slip.
The faucet turns on
With a breath or a sigh.
We live and we die.

Slide through the day
A lifetime appears.
The doorbell rings.
It's you in old age.
When that faucet drips,
Take smaller sips.

THE FORGERY

It was not written down.
It was not in a letter.
A mouth became a tool,
A kiss, but so much better.

The key was in the touch.
Soft feathers in a nest.
A pacifying pause,
Just a tantalizing test.

Feelings falsified.
Like flying way too high,
Plummeting to earth,
Then...caught

In another lie

PEACE

And there it is...
Stark, static,
pristine particles
dancing in your eyes,
counterclockwise.

Non-thinking,
like death in absentia.
A bodiless pacifier
trimmed in blacklight.
Heaven, but not quite.

Looking out and in.
Transparent time
with no recall.
Nothing, nothing
at all.
Eating pablum,
with a steady hum.

NAKED

The watermelon rind was left
Juices plucked and eaten
It was green and seedless
Like her hollowness
That feeling of lost control
No longer whole

The platter was white
Washed and put away
Spotless once again
Ready for more fruit
A taste to recapture
That ripe random rapture
But...the rind was still bare

FLIGHT

Feathers fly
From windblown birds
And scatter thoughts
Like tragedies
Deep inside
The song is heard
Nature sings
soliloquies

We do not hear
The whistled note
A lilting cry
Of endless night
But then our souls
Are intertwined
With sun and soil
in final flight

OVERFLOW

Bubbles pop one by one
Like the froth on top of beer
A flowing-over of a liquid stream
Dribbling down the glass
A connection with the frozen ice
That tingling feeling in the skin
Ideas born within

The steady flow circulates
As the drink shifts the mind
Like pouring it in a larger glass
While ordering a shot of rum
It burns but churns internally
And swims inside the blood
Until there is a flood...

TURBULENCE

A slow fire in a tossed salad
Where every movement cries
Burning muscles collide
Like cream that starts to curdle
With buzzing nerves inside

Waves of pain in a marathon
Start vibrating in every vein
A clamor of aching tantrums
Screams and pounds in rage
The body no longer hums

It is just the quaking of age

THE WAITING ROOM

Confinement in a room
Time trapped in cages
A book with no pages

Reading out loud
In silent wonder
But inward thunder

A home with one exit
Here we dwell
Perhaps this is Hell

The door never opens
Windowless waiting
For something

...Maybe nothing

BLENDED

The rocket strayed
Off course

Strange creatures
Red raspberry hair
Thin dangling arms
Translucent skins
But smiling eyes
With twisted grins

How unlike we were
Dark oval faces
Blue hands and feet
Sad pouting lips
We did not stare
We did not care

Peace overdo
Just blending...
With a different hue

FACES

A crowd formed
Scattering began
Faces forming
Frowns brooding
Smiling secrets
Worried creases

What lies behind
External expressions?
Wonder and worry
Desire and dreams
They all go home
We are left alone

Looking in the mirror,
We also ask
What do WE mask?

THE GRAYING

Long ago but yesterday
Time moved too fast
Playing hide and seek
Thoughts are hiding now
Seeking words forgotten
A life game we call "how?"

Flashlight tag in the dark
A slow waltz down the hill
The graying of the day
A backward glance appeal
Meandering in the mind
The turning of the wheel

ERASER

The word was erased
So now there was a hole
Like an open window
With a view to the outside
She had pressed too hard
Too vigorously
So now the story ended
This is not what she intended

One word replaced
Would have made it complete
But the Eraser was strong
And she wanted nothing wrong

She could see beyond
A tale seen through a keyhole
Like a telescopic lens
Observing more than expected
It was a view of life itself
Not like the fiction she had tried
So... she crawled inside
To the outside

THE CLOSING

The wind sang and the breeze sighed
A musical wind chime of joy
Summer senses felt the change,
Breathing in the blossomed buds
As the sun and clouds interchanged
Bare feet, no socks, no need to hide
For those who cannot climb the hills,
As old age slows them down
To bend the knee in gardening,
Is as painful as lost youth
They still have portals that open wide
To a world that's called "outside."

But some of us are windowless
And some have closed their doors,
Their songs are now unsung
They forgot they once were young

THE ITCH

Sitting still was not easy
Things began to twitch
They pinched her skin,
Bit her feet and crawled within

Invisible creatures screamed
Burrowed deeper as she sat
She wanted to scratch
Before they could hatch

It was finally just too late
Covered in prickly pleas
Like a burn from too much sun
She knew what had to be done

That itch is in everyone
But much more in some

THE LAST DROP

There was no list
No specific time
The stars still far away
The ground too deep and cold
It was warm inside her nest
Tomorrow came and went
Like water inside a cup
Something she could hold

Water can be contained
But eventually evaporate
Surrounding her life with cups,
She poured her years inside,
Never missing one last drop
She wanted death to wait
So she never drank too fast
She wanted life to last...

TIME FREEZE

A puzzle in motion
A roller skate day
Green and golden
The pieces all fit
Easy to wander
But better to stay

A raspberry treasure
Bubblegum breeze
It all came together
A time to remember
The popsicle picnic
An ice cream freeze

Melting moments
Dripping in the heat
We tried to savor
All of the flavor
A delicious delight
...Take another bite

SURROGATE BEAUTY

Looking in behind the eye
Into the world of self
Purple veins twist and turn
A jungle of nerves and bones
Raw and ragged heart beats
But to her, it is a garden
Her variegated lie

A masterpiece creation
Of vital liquid rose
Vibrant branches blooming
Planting as she goes
Beauty lives inside her
She may be close to dying
But her imagination grows

HELP...

Slow motion desperation
Like a crumpled wad of paper
An exhale in slow motion
Sinking in the quicksand
But so slowly you can float
No desire to surrender
Yet unable to cope
Please...throw me a rope

INSIDE

The space inside your brain
Where life resides
Sometimes pauses
A frozen centrifuge
Where blood is solidified
A breach deep inside

No one sees that halt
That twirling mass
Orbiting in frenzied ire
A plethora of panic and fears
That lives and breathes
Except it leaks...
In tears

FANTASIZE

The long list of living
Like birds on a wire
Or trains on a track
We watch them fly by
Unable to slow them down
Helpless and fragile
Feathers and freight
All we can do is wait

In the meantime:
Hang from the wire
Jump on the train
Make things a fantasy
Pretend and create
Your mind still moves
Set yourself free
Now...
Go climb a tree

FROZEN AFFINITY

Parallel lines never intersect
They travel along in equality
Partners in patterns
Poetic perfection
But something is missing...
Lips never kissing

Touch not existing
No warmth, heat or flame
Like shelves in a freezer
Or an echo in motion
Frozen affinity in space
Love...without a face

ECLIPSE

Men hollow and hungry
Swallowed the sun
They thought they won
But the luster dimmed
And dark words spoke

A blather of ignorance
Obtuse and obscure
Mouths full of doubt
Perhaps they should spit
The light back out...

BARRICADE

The wispy wanderings
Warped her mind
Cobwebs and cotton balls
Pieces of fluff
Strands and fibers
Filagree fingers
That rearranged stuff

Threading a needle
With feathers and fur
Strands of strings
Tangled and frayed
In a mental blockade
She created the mess
To forget and regress

HERE

Above the open skylight
Beyond the every day
Under the midnight after
Below the flower garden
Upon the horizontal tray

Always somewhere else
To find the tools we need
To dig and plant the laughter
Inside our troubled souls
And grow the needed seed

We always wonder where?
It's just...over there

THE DIRGE

That trembling raspy riot
That never seemed to cease
Bounced around the halls
And ricocheted the walls

An empty chamber haunted
By the dirge of rattling chains
A cough is caustic stuff
And the body says "enough"

THE STRANGER

Looking in was like a door in the woods
A shocking confrontation with the absurd
There was no explanation for it
It was not a familiar sight
Opening the door would not be right

Like a stranger walking in your home
You do not recognize the face
Entering was never an invitation
And yet, you had to look inside
The mirror -
A door to what you hide

AWAKENING

A picture in a frame
Gray guardian of life
A moment memorized
A time immortalized

The scene was black and white
An old house in a field
A structure gone awry
An awakening of the eye

Open up the door
Paint the walls bright red
Create a spiral stair
See what isn't there

The picture comes alive
Construct what might have been
The mind can color and blend
Possibilities never end...

RAIN

It was raining inside
The liquid seeped from pores
Nothing could stop the dripping
Like a gargoyle,
Tortured stone above a castle,
Water spouting from its mouth
As it remained motionless
Steadfast and stoic

A type of weeping in a storm
The thunder of remorse
The lightning of recall
When bullets did not rain
And stone figures did not cry
What can be done
To make us see
We've lost our empathy?

RED BIRD

The invisible girl joined the crowd
She stood and listened
Her mantle glowed softly
Perhaps that's all they saw
A red coat

She could move in and out
Always on the fringe
Never recognized
But she heard their voices
Knew their plans

That was her life
Like a small bird in a tree
Foliage covering her nest
As her coat changed
Camouflaged...she thought

But they knew she was there
They needed her
That presence of stability,
Hearing what she had not said
And were thankful for...

The girl in red

3 AM THEATER

The light is on within and without
Time to wander in mental space
Bubbles of inspiration and rhyme
Suspend the concept of time
That non verbal Theater begins
There the colors blend
One word creates a stage
Action on a page

Endless stories are told
As the images unfold
The scenes are all behind
The curtain of your mind

THE LOOKING GLASS

The window was smudged
A portent picture in dust
It resembled a tree
A willow with bent arms
And black rotting bark
The image was stark

It was a cryptic combination
Of reflective foreshadowing
An austere arrangement
With an eerie prophesy
And yet, some saw beauty
Alluring artistry

Looking out or looking in,
We see...what we want to see

THE SHOE

She jumped on the train
One foot still hanging
Her shoe hung from her toe
And there it is,
Life's refrain

Tracks do not waver
Just follow along
But what of the shoe?
That pendulous thing
The song that we sing

Does she travel alone
Or remember what's gone?
Lyrics that linger,
Like a suspended shoe,
Reminders
Of what we once knew

INK SPOT

Far deep in the pen
Was a secret
A thought
One that emerged
You never knew when

Like a bullet
In the barrel of a gun
Black and bedeviled
It bubbled and churned
Cooled and then burned

One click and a shot:
A wondrous reply,
A sordid goodbye,
A life or death plea
A dire decree

...And all from a spot

PEELING

Pull the box top to see inside
Smooth the baggie to close it tight
Say the words to open her heart
Tiptoe softly and close the door
Peel away the outer shell
There you'll find the inner core

The pearl that forms
Wisdom we've learned

Stored away in the back of our soul
Old letters found in an antique drawer
It takes so long to pull them out
Hidden within, there's always more

CRESCENDO

The notes ran sideways and hid
They were chased by discord
A medley of deceit played on
Raucous rhythms rallied
And an atonal chord began

It was a time of the downbeat
Where a solo would not do
An entire orchestra was needed
To create a bridge

Perhaps an ensemble in key
Would compose a resolution,
A new tempo, loud and clear
In perfect harmony

THREADBARE

The scissors...
Bent and broken
Too many edges frayed
Corners raveled away
Patterns torn to shreds
Nothing left to say

Like pages pulled apart
Ragged words hang loose
Dangling by a thread
Stagnant disarray
Tattered fringe swaying
In a suspended mute ballet

BLUE DIALOGUE

Raptured thoughts stuck above
Hovered there like a question mark
No place to go - no way down
"What's next?
Heaven, Hell or in between?
Do we linger if not seen?"

Just the soul - a blue balloon
The shadowed part
Lyrics left inside the brain
Wet pavement after rain
"Where do we go
When life dries up?"

A voice replied:
"Your sun has set
So now you are...
The afterglow"

LISTEN

Ticking tales go on and on
Time bombs in lullabies
They wander in the woods
Shift and stir with the wind
While others wait and watch
Heed the finite murmurs
The whispers in the earth
Thunder tells a story
A sigh, a secret truth
Quiet is a quandary
Silence is misread

Listen...
to what's not said

DREAM

Sit for a while
Close all the doors
Expand a mystery
Rustic realms reappear
Vistas that could be

Purple plans in the tree
Whimsical windows open
The world is widened
One branch at a time
Captured transparency

Wink at the wonder
See deep inside
A porcelain potpourri
Madness and sadness
Red reality

Disappear...
Magically

KERFUFFLE

The world of empty
Filled back up
Flung its contents
Into the rain
Wet and weathered
The pieces flew
Paper shreds,
Like summer snow,
Plastered the windows
Stuck to the doors
Life was covered
With garbage and lies
Forget the mess
Ignore the flies
Close your eyes

ANGRY HORN

Blasted black eyes
Shivered through the tube
Projecting pity

It shifted focus
Tore through the skin
And settled in the heart

It pulsated dark matter
An explosive orb
Of sound

A screaming horn
Reverberating
In a hole

Touching the soul...

THE TRANSFER

Timid eyes squint and strain
But miss the dancing danger.
Specks spray like ballet twirls.
They land on slippery floors.
Pointed shoes direct the way
But the droplets do not stay.

They pass to partners,
Prance and spin,
Collide like acrobats.
The audience is unaware
The transfer has begun
And, for some, their dance
Is done!

FLOATING

Levitating in water
A jello float
No sound
But a muffled voice
A ghost whispering
Through a straw

Beneath the clock
Above the time
Sliding in a space
Somewhere
In between
Peace prevails

A transitory balance
Of buoyancy

DARK CHOCOLATE

Deep down in a box
Under black paper
There was an eye
A red wanderer
Waiting

Layered cordials
Covered closed lids
But not asleep
Chocolate shields
Knew what to hide

Delicious delicacy
The cherry of life
Bitten in half
To find out
What's inside

FELLOW TRAVELERS

Get in
The door is open
You are safe
The bullets fall
But not in here
I travel on
With you inside
Away from fear

But other souls
Are now with us
Curled in shadows
Sleeping still
Memories...
They travel too
Until our journey's
Through

THE POET'S EYE

Everything in the sea
Collects in me
A silver spoon
The moon
Ants in the sand
Veins in a hand

The ceiling slips
Becomes the floor
I walk on beams
To find the door
Open
There's always more

I breathe in oceans
And drink the breeze
Hear the silence
Then shut the door
My mind is stuffed
With poetic fluff

But...
It's never
Enough!

ABOUT THE AUTHOR

Kathy Kuzma is a retired teacher who lives in the country with her husband, two cats and three dogs. Her love of nature is relevant to all aspects of life. After obtaining a bachelor's degree in English from Wayne State University, Kathy went on to receive her master's degree in Special Education from Oakland University. She taught at the secondary level in English and Special Education and became a Teacher Consultant at the elementary level. Kathy has written 3 other books of poetry and two children's books. They are on Barnes & Noble and Amazon.com.

Her pen name is Katje Kaase and her web site is www.kkuzma.com

Printed in the United States
by Baker & Taylor Publisher Services